M<

Manipulation

How to Train Your Brain to Think Faster, Concentrate More, and Remember Anything

T. Whitmore

Table of Contents

INTRODUCTION

Do you consider yourself forgetful and would need help in improving your memory? Are you worried because you tend to forget even the simplest things?

Before you panic, what I want you to understand is forgetting things is a usual part of life. Think of your brain as a storage space and the information or memories are the files that you store in them. Our brain has the capacity to accumulate information and store it in our memory for a certain period of time. Those memories that our brain deems not-so-important will be lost, those that are important will be filed in another storage space where we can retrieve the information when we need it. There are many reasons why we forget, and I will discuss further about that later, but without our brain's ability to sort out all of the information we encode in it, our memory would be overloaded with information that we don't even need.

Don't get me wrong, I'm not saying that being forgetful is OK, what I'm trying to point out is that forgetfulness is really a part of everyday life. Forgetting where you placed the keys, overlooking what you need to do next, and experiencing the "tip of the tongue moments" are all normal. However, if forgetfulness is already affecting your life, for example:

forgetting important dates, having a hard time recalling names of your relatives, or forgetting your home address, then those are the red flags that your memory may be deteriorating.

Whether you're already in your twilight years and is already experiencing memory lapses, or you just want to improve your memory to do better in school or at work, the good thing is that you have the ability to increase your brain's ability no matter what age you are! Several studies show that the brain has the ability called *neuroplasticity* where it can adapt to change no matter what age you are. That means, even if you start exercising your brain as an adult, your memory can still be improved; and I will show you how in this book.

Before I go on any further, I'd like to thank you and congratulate you for downloading this book, "Memory Manipulation". In this book, you will learn more than just strategies on improving the memory since I dedicated the first chapter of the book explaining the human memory and how the memory process works. There's also a chapter that will discuss the different causes of memory loss. This is important to know so that you will be able to avoid them. There is also a chapter that discusses the different lifestyle changes and even diet that you can follow to improve and strengthen your memory. Finally, there's a chapter that is the meat of this book which will discuss different techniques like *chunking, association,* and *mnemonics* to help improve your memory.

It's never too late or too early to improve your memory, move to the first chapter now! Happy reading!

Chapter 1: The Human Memory Explained

For centuries, experts have been trying to figure out what the memory is, how it works, and why we forget. In the past, scientists pictured the human memory as a huge filing cabinet where information is stored and retrieved when needed. Some describe the brain as a library where memories are stored on book shelves, or even a supercomputer where a huge load of data can be stored and recovered. Recent studies show that the memory is more complicated than that. In fact, the memory is not a part of your body (like your arms, nose, eyes, lips, etc.), but is a **brain-wide process** that enables us to remember or recall information, situations, or experiences given the right stimulus. Scientists now describe the memory like a complex web of connections (known as *synapses*) that are spread all throughout the brain. These connections grow stronger over time, especially when we experience things that are related to these memories or information. Even our senses are involved in creating memories. Our memories aren't formed merely by seeing or hearing information, it involves using the different senses as well.

For example, if I were to ask you to describe your memory of Christmas mornings, how would you describe it? For me, my

Christmas morning memory would involve the feeling of excitement as I tear open the wrapped gifts under the tree, it also involves smelling the delicious chocolate chip and banana pancakes my mom used to make for Christmas mornings, and it also includes the sound of the Christmas songs my father used to play on his stereo.

Our memory is more than just recalling what you reviewed the night before the exam, and it's also more than remembering the telephone number of the pizza delivery nearby. Being able to remember helps us grow and learn from our past experiences, and it also allows us to adapt to present situations. You have to understand that our memory is vital everyday living.

Do you think you could last a day without your memory? How can you drive to work from your home if you can't remember the directions? How will you be able to finish important tasks if you forget them? Or, how will you be able to learn new things at school or in the office without your memory? It's totally impossible!

That's why, it's important that you keep your memory in its top shape. Keep in mind that the brain is like a muscle, when you use it daily and exercise it, it will grow and become stronger. However, if you fail to use it, especially when you grow older, your brain turns weak, which will make learning and memorizing harder.

"There are so many reasons to train your brain and to keep it sharp as a knife. Mental health, happiness, peace of mind, and the quality of your life. You'll find continuous brain training is what sets the stage for keeping focus and memory well into old age. It seems so obvious; there's no need to explain. Because everybody knows, no train, no gain," says brain trainer Steven L. Snyder in one of his published interviews online.

It's never too late to improve and strengthen your memory, and I will show you how on Chapter 3. First, you have to understand how the brain is able to create, store, and retrieve memory.

THE MEMORY PROCESSES

Like I said earlier, our memory is not a body part, but is a complex process. Even though our memory is complex, the process itself could be divided into three other processes— **encoding, storage,** and **retrieval** (also called as recall).

Encoding

Encoding is the first and most crucial process of creating a memory. It refers to the step in which an *item* (it could be an information, an experience, etc.) would be transformed by the brain into what experts call as a *construct* that would be stored and eventually retrieved from the memory.

Studies explain that we are able to encode experiences or information by perceiving it through our senses—our sense of sight, smell, sound, taste, and touch. For example, when you are trying to memorize a written speech, your eyes (visual encoding) and ears (acoustic encoding) are able to encode this information to the brain. This data would then go to the part of the brain called the hippocampus, which has the responsibility of binding all these items into a single memory. After this, the memory would then travel to two other parts of the brain, which is the frontal cortex and amygdala before it is successfully stored in your memory.

Experts believe that the likelihood of information to be encoded in the brain will be based on the emotion and attention that we have during the experience. This explains why we often remember things that interest us, or caused us to be emotional.

Storage

Storage is the second process in which the new information is filtered into three different "compartments" categorized as the **sensory memory, short-term memory,** and **long-term memory.**

Sensory memory could be described as the compartment in which the information is stored the shortest. It refers to our ability to retain certain data that we encoded through our senses without us paying close attention to it. For example, as you drive by an alley you see a person wearing a red shirt crossing the street. Although this experience could be stored your sensory memory, it would only be retained in the memory very briefly.

Often referred to as the "brain's Post-it Note" the **short-term memory** is the compartment where an information can be stored around 10 to 15 seconds before the memory is lost. The short term memory for example, enables you to memorize a telephone number before typing it in your smartphone. It also allows you to recall what your boss is asking you to do before you can write it down on paper. Unfortunately, any information that our brains stores in the short-term memory could be lost unless you put a conscious effort to retain the memory, or if that information is often used.

Finally, the **long-term memory** refers to the compartment in which information is stored for a long period of time. Some even argue that even as we age, and experience frequent memory lapses, the information that are stored in the long-term memory are there to stay. Those data stored in the short-term memory can become a long term memory through a technique called consolidation that involves repetition and association of the information.

The kind of stimuli in which the information was encoded would determine on what compartment it would be stored. Without the brain's ability to compartmentalize the experiences we encounter every day, our brain would go into an information overload.

Retrieval

This part of the memory process is when we try to access or remember the information that was successfully encoded and stored in our memory. Retrieval enables us to recall important dates such as anniversaries, birthdays, etc. It also allows us to remember names of the people that we usually encounter.

Although retrieval allows us to recall the things that are important as well as the significant events that happened to us, you have to take note that not all memories are accurate. In fact, these memories could be altered by the current situation we are in.

Retrieval of our memory could also be difficult, especially when an old memory is replaced with a new one, or when information decays or fades overtime that causes us to forget.

Chapter 2: Causes of Memory Loss

Like I said in the introduction, forgetting things is a usual part of life. However, even though it is inevitable to forget, it doesn't mean that you should not do anything in order to lessen it. It seems like forgetting where you placed your keys is harmless, but a usual occurrence of this could mean that you're wasting a lot of time just trying to look for them. Also, missing out on a special occasion just because you forgot about it, might also affect your relationship with other people. Even with these simple illustrations, you could clearly how important improving your memory is. But before we get into the techniques to strengthen your memory, you must first understand what causes us to forget.

Some experts believe that memories aren't lost, but instead we find it hard to retrieve the information encoded and stored in our memory. While others believe that memories decay and are lost overtime, especially when it is not important information. But whatever explanation you want to believe in, the bottom line is that forgetfulness can affect your life, and that it has quite a lot of causes; some of them are:

1. **Lack of attention**— Why can't you recall the person's name who was just introduced to you? One of the reasons why you can't remember his name is because you didn't pay close attention when he was introduced to you.

2.

   Like I mentioned earlier, information can only be stored in the long-term memory if there was high emotion involved or if we made the conscious effort to really remember the information. Because if you lacked attention on something, this means that either your brain didn't encode anything, or it was just stored in the sensory memory.

3. **Interference**—Psychologists from the 1930s to the 1950s believe that one of the major causes of forgetfulness is interference. They theorized that people find it hard to recall a past memory when it is interfered with a new one or vice versa. For example, for the past year, you've been trying to learn how to speak the Japanese language and then the following year, you decided to learn the Korean language. However, when you met individuals who spoke Japanese, you found it hard recalling the terms you learned in the past because

it is already replaced or interfered with a new language that you learned.

4. **The information wasn't stored in your long-term memory**— Another reason why we sometimes forget is because some memories are only stored in the short-term memory (which can only last 10-15 seconds) rather than the long-term memory.

Was there a time when you actually had to repeat looking at an address just so you can mentally memorize it? Don't worry if you find it hard memorizing it the first time. That's just your brain deciding that this information is only good in your short-term memory and not in the long-term memory. However, with constant exercise, you will find yourself easily memorizing and remembering these things with the use of memory techniques which I will share with you later.

5. **The connections in our brain weakens**— According to the Decay Theory, the connections or what is called the synapses can weaken overtime if an

information isn't often used or retrieved. When these connections decay, we will find it hard to retrieve the information making us experience what is known as the "tip of the tongue moments".

6. **Traumatic experiences**—Even though emotions could help us store experiences and information in the long-term memory, some situations that are too extreme could lead someone to experience Dissociative Amnesia. People who undergo traumatic experiences such as natural calamities, accidents, abuse, and war can make a person forget his or her past experiences as well as some important information. This type of memory loss is serious and should be addressed with the help of an expert.

7. **Medications**— Studies show that people who are under medications such as anti-depressants, sleeping pills, and drugs to manage hypertension can experience memory loss as well as confusion.

8. **Sleep Apnea**— This refers to a sleep disorder in which a person briefly stops breathing throughout his sleep.

Although this condition is treatable, people who don't address sleep apnea could also experience memory loss, as well as dementia. A research found in the Journal of Neuroscience says that this condition directly affects what you call the *spatial navigation memory* that helps us to recall directions and where we placed things.

9. **Too much stress or anxiety**— Besides the physical pain you feel when you have high levels or anxiety or stress, you will also have a hard time concentrating and receiving new information. Keep in mind that in order for information to be encoded and stored in your memory, you need to pay close attention to it; stress and anxiety just make it hard for you to concentrate, and much more difficult for you to remember new information.

10. **Depression**— If left untreated, depression could directly affect a person's brain function. Not only will the individual have mood swings, lose interest in daily activities, but his/her memory will also be affected.

11. **Drinking too much alcohol—** Ever wondered why you can't remember what happened last night after you got drunk? That's because drinking too much alcohol than what is recommended (2 bottles of beer for men, 1 bottle for women) could affect a person's short-term memory. Besides that, a study from the American Academy of Neurology reported that individuals who were abusive in drinking alcohol had symptoms of cognitive decline earlier than those who were only light drinkers.

12. **Aging—**Many believe that memory lapses are always a part of growing old. Although a lot of older adults have troubles remembering things because of cognitive deterioration, it doesn't mean that it's inevitable. Like I said, you can keep your brain and memory healthy as long as you exercise and strengthen it every day.

13. **Other serious health conditions—** Besides aging and the ones I mentioned above, another reason why people experience memory loss is because they could be suffering from other health conditions that affect the memory; some of these health conditions are:

- **Amnesia—** A person with this condition can experience a loss in their memory for a long period of time. There are two types of amnesia: anterograde and retrograde. An individual with an anterograde amnesia will have difficulties creating new memories, while a person with retrograde amnesia will have trouble recalling his/her existing memories. Head injuries, illnesses, as well as substance abuse are some of the causes of amnesia.

- **Dementia—** Because of the deterioration of brain cells that happens to people who have dementia, they will have problems with their short-term memory. This means that people with dementia will have difficulty in remembering what just recently happened. Besides this, symptoms such as confusion, mood swings, and difficulties in accomplishing day to day tasks will be harder for them. Statistics show that adults who are 65 and above are those who are prone to dementia; however, it could still be avoided if you keep your brain healthy and memory sharp.

- **Alzheimer's Disease**— This is the most common type of dementia that directly affects a person's memory. Unfortunately, millions of people are affected with this disease (44 million, according to Alzheimer's Disease International). People with Alzheimer's disease will have a hard time creating new memories, and eventually would also lose their long-term memories. The latter stages of this disease could also make a person find it hard to do easy tasks such as taking a bath, brushing their teeth, and even eating.

- **Korsakoff Syndrome**— Defined as a chronic memory disorder, the Korsakoff Syndrome is caused by the deficiency of thiamine in the body. A person with this disorder could suffer the same condition as a person with dementia.

- **Parkinson's Disease**— Caused by the deterioration of the neurons in a region of the brain called the substantia nigra, a person with Parkinson's Disease could have difficulty in his motor skills. Although this disease could primarily affect the patient's motor control, individuals who suffer Parkinson's Disease are also prone to developing dementia which affects their brain and memory.

Although there are quite a lot of reasons why people forget or experience memory loss, what I want you to understand is that these could be prevented or addressed if you keep your brain healthy and make sure that you exercise it daily to maintain your memory sharp; even at old age. Turn to the page to discover ways on how you can improve your memory!

CHAPTER 3: MEMORY IMPROVEMENT TECHNIQUES

Ever wish you had a sharp memory so that you always aced the test that required you to memorize hundreds of facts and figures? Or are you tired of always forgetting things and then wasting time looking for it? Well, the good news is that you have the power to stretch your brain and improve your memory through techniques and exercising it daily.

Whether your purpose of reading this book is to improve your memory to be better at school or work, or just simply lessen your memory lapses, the memory improvement techniques that I will share with you in this chapter are proven to be effective to help sharpen your memory through constant practice.

One of the most common memory tools is *mnemonics*. These are different types of devices or techniques that will enable you to remember or recall even a huge chunk of information through lists, words, acronyms, etc. According to a study in the 1960's by Gerald R. Miller, a University professor in the US, students who often used mnemonics in learning had an impressive 77% increase in their test scores, which proves that this technique is very helpful to improve your memory.

ACRONYMS

This is the most basic technique that you can use to recall a list or a larger piece of information. By using acronyms, you just simply take the first letter of each word in the list to easily remember the information.

For example, you have to memorize the how you can treat a sprain, in order to make memorizing easier for you, just remember the acronyms letters: **RICE** which means: **R**est injured area, **I**ce the sprain, **C**ompress with a bandage, and **E**levate the injured area.

Other common examples of acronyms are: **NASA**- **N**ational **A**eronautics, and **S**pace **A**dministration, **NBA**- **N**ational **B**asketball **A**ssociation, and **WHO**- **W**orld **H**ealth **O**rganization.

NAME MNEMONIC

Like the acronyms, what you need to do in order to use this technique is to take the first letters of each word in the list, but the difference is that you can re-arrange (unless you need it in order) the list to create a name that you can easily recall. Some of the best examples of this are: **Roy G. Biv** that stands for the colors of the rainbow: **R**ed, **O**range, **G**reen, **B**lue, **I**ndigo, and **V**iolet or **Pvt. Tim Hall**, that stands for the complete list of amino acids: **P**henylalanine, **V**aline, **T**hreonine, **T**ryptophan, **I**soleucine, **M**ethionine, **H**istidine, **A**rginine, **L**eucine, and **L**ysine.

Although using acronyms and name mnemonics are very helpful in remembering a number of information, they are only good for "rote learning" where you are able to recall or remember information only through repetition. But it doesn't mean that you comprehend the context of the information that you're trying to remember. So even if these two are very helpful, keep in mind that comprehending and understanding the information is still the best way to learn and remember.

ACROSTICS/SENTENCE MNEMONICS

Just like the first two techniques, you will also use the first letters of each word in the list. However, instead of forming a word or a name using these letters, you will use them in order to make a sentence.

For example, in order to remember the order of operations in math, which is: **P**arentheses, **E**xponents, **M**ultiply, **D**ivide, **A**dd, and **S**ubtract, you can turn its acronym **PEMDAS** into a sentence mnemonic: **P**lease **E**xcuse **M**y **D**ear **A**unt **S**ally. Or when you're trying to remember the nine planets of the solar system which is: **M**ercury, **V**enus, **E**arth, **M**ars, **J**upiter, **S**aturn, **U**ranus, **N**eptune, and **P**luto, and use the **MVEMJSUNP** acronym to: **M**y **V**ery **E**xcited **M**other **J**ust **S**erved **U**s **N**ine **P**izzas.

SONGS MNEMONICS

This is a type of mnemonic technique where you use music, or particularly the melody of a song you know well in order to memorize information. For example, some kindergarten classes in the US use the melody of the ABC song in order to sing and recite the 50 states of America. In Sunday school, they teach children the Books of the Bible Song in order to help them memorize the 27 books of the New Testament.

CHUNKING

This type of technique is ideal for recalling digits, mastering this will help you to remember telephone numbers easily.

Chunking is based on the idea that you could only keep a limited number of information in the short-term memory for a very brief period of time. According to studies, most people can memorize more or less seven numbers or items, which is very helpful, since most telephone numbers come in seven digits. *But how come do you still have a hard time memorizing phone numbers?* Maybe because you're not chunking!

Try memorizing this in 5 seconds: **8610907**

Are you able to memorize it?

What about this? **861-0907**

I'm sure that you were able to memorize the second one faster and better, that's because you "chunked" the numbers into smaller groups which is easier for you to remember.

VISUALIZATION AND ASSOCIATION

Besides mnemonics, of the best memory improvement techniques are visualization and association. That's because most people can memorize better when they visualize the information that they're trying to learn.

To use this technique, you simply have to follow three basic steps, which are: substitute words, visualize a vivid image, and lastly, associate these images together.

For example, you're trying to learn the islands in the Caribbean, however you always forget about Montserrat and its capital, Plymouth. In order to keep this in mind, you can follow the steps of the visualization and association technique.

Step 1: Substitute Words

Since Plymouth, Montserrat is a hard term to remember, what you need to do is to substitute these terms simpler words.

Take Plymouth for example, what words can you replace that are easy to remember, but sounds like Plymouth? What I can think of is for Plymouth is a fly (ply) and a mouth (mouth).

Now, what about the island, Montserrat? The only thing that I could think of is to replace Montserrat is monster rat.

Step 2: Visualize a Vivid Image

After substituting the words, the next thing you need to do is to create a clear, mental picture of it. Now, what I can imagine is a fly with a big mouth and a humongous and scary monster rat. (The bigger and more vivid your mental image is, the better)

Step 3: Associate the Images Together

In order for you to associate Plymouth and Montserrat together, what you need to do now is to associate the two images together, or place them in one big scene. For me, the next time I have to recall what the capital of Montserrat is, I'll visualize a scary monster rat trying to catch a fly with a big mouth (Plymouth, Montserrat).

Don't be worried if you substitute words that seem odd or create a vivid image that is silly (like my example). That's because the sillier and more odd the image is in your memory, the better you can recall them.

MINDFULNESS

Finally, another technique that could help you improve your memory is practicing mindfulness. Mindfulness is defined as "the state of being conscious or aware of something". It means that you are aware of thoughts, emotions, and the things happening around you at the present moment. Practicing mindfulness enables you to be "in the now"; far from the thoughts that take you away from what's happening to you at the moment.

How can being "in the now" help improve memory? Like what I said in the previous chapter, the information that you want keep in your memory can only be stored if you pay close attention to it. Things that seem passive and are not repeatedly remembered will only end up in the sensory memory or the short-term memory. However, if you want important details to remain in your long-term memory, what you need to do is to be mindful—to give full attention to what you are trying to learn.

Practicing mindfulness teaches you to tame down the "noise" or different thoughts in your head that is pulling your attention from the present moment.

Having problems recalling the names of the people you just met? By being mindful when you are meeting and conversing with other people, you are able to take in all of the information presented to you without any distractions. Since your focus is there, it is more likely that these experiences will get encoded in your brain, which will help you recall the names of the people you're talking to.

Are you always misplacing things like your keys or phone? Mindfulness will help you to remember where you placed the things that are important because you are fully aware of everything you do and the things that are happening to you at the moment.

Now that you learned some of the most effective memory techniques, I challenge you to try them yourselves. It will take some time for you to master them, but you'll surely find them very effective and helpful in sharpening your memory.

CHAPTER 4: THINGS YOU CAN DO TO KEEP IMPROVING MEMORY AND PREVENT MEMORY LOSS

Besides the techniques I shared with you in the previous chapter, there are also some activities and lifestyle changes you can do in order to improve your memory and prevent memory loss.

If you want to keep your memory sharp what you need to understand is that you have to take conscious effort to train your brain to make it stronger. Like a muscle the brain can only become stronger through exercises. Even if you're already an adult, you can begin training your brain daily through different brain exercises. Some of the activities you can do are:

- **Crosswords Puzzles or Sudoku**

-

    Go ahead and buy yourself a crossword puzzle or Sudoku book, or try ones that are free online. Make this a routine in order to continually stimulate your brain, and at the same time increase your know-how in general knowledge. An article from the website of the Alzheimer's Association reports that there are studies that say that keeping the brain active through activities such as crossword puzzles and Sudoku can "increase the brain's vitality and may build its reserves of brain cells and connections."

- **Test Your Memory**

If puzzles aren't your thing, maybe you can do a simple brain exercise such as trying to memorize a list and recalling it later. You can use your grocery list to do this. Try to remember the items on your list, and then after an hour, try to recall the items again. This simple activity will stimulate your brain and would help improve your memory over time.

- **Skip the Calculator**

Although it's easier to compute using a calculator on your smartphone, it would be great for your brain and memory if you challenge yourself to compute math mentally. You can even further test yourself by taking math problems and solving them "old school style"— using a pen and paper.

- **Learn a New Language**

Not only will you increase your skills, but you will also stimulate your brain, which can help strengthen the memory. In fact, a study published on sciencedaily.com, showed that people who have a rich vocabulary have lesser tendencies to experience cognitive decline when they get older.

- **Consider Enrolling in a Cooking Class**

Since the senses play a big role in encoding information and experiences to the brain, one activity you can do in order to sharpen your memory is to enroll in a cooking class since cooking involves almost all the senses such as taste, smell, touch and sight.

- **Learn to Play an Instrument**

Never think that you're old enough to learn new things. Keep in mind that as long as you live, your brain has the ability to adapt and learn new things such as playing an instrument. Again, like the other brain exercises, learning to play the guitar, for instance, will help stimulate the brain and improve memory since learning this will require using your senses such as touch and hearing.

- **Read, Read, and Read!**

Another simple activity that you can do in order to keep your brain busy is to read books, newspapers, or other references as much as you can. Reading stories help ignite your imagination which also prevents memory loss.

Besides the activities that I mentioned above, there are also some lifestyle changes you need to make in order to boost the brain's function and improve your memory. Some of these are:

- **Get Enough Sleep**

Having a busy schedule and tons of tasks that you need to accomplish could really deprive you from having a good night's sleep. However, even though you feel like you can survive with less than 5 hours of sleep, it doesn't mean that it's doing any good for your health, including your brain's function. If you want to improve your memory, then you must make sure that you have at least 7-9 hours of quality sleep every night. That's because when we're asleep, our brain is working to store information and experiences in our memory. By depriving yourself from sleep, your neurons will develop slowly making focusing and retrieving memories harder.

- **Exercise**

You're totally wrong to think that exercising is only for your physical body. Research shows that exercising, even 30 minutes to an hour everyday can help improve the brain's function. It is also believed that regular exercise can tremendously decrease the chances of developing diseases that can cause you to lose your memory. An expert from Georgetown University Medical Center said that regular physical exercise is best to preserve the brain's function and memory even with aging.

- **Learn How to Manage Stress**

Like I said earlier, anxiety and stress can cause someone to have attention difficulties and also experience memory loss. Not only that, chronic stress can also lead to depression which can again impair the memory. In order to avoid this along with the other complications that come with stress, you should learn how to manage it.

Know when you need to take a breather during a hectic day, take day offs to clear your mind from stress, and if needed, seek help from professionals.

- **Turn Away from Your Vices**

You may think that smoking can only cause damage to your lungs, but that's totally wrong. In fact, a study in a university in England showed that smokers actually lose a third of their memory daily as an effect of smoking. However, people who were able to quit smoking were able to regain the levels of their memory like those who were non-smokers.

Drinking excessively on the other hand can also impair one's memory. Alcoholism can also cause you to develop the Korsakoff Syndrome, which is a neurological disorder that has the same symptoms as with dementia.

- **Be Connected with Loved Ones**

Studies prove that individuals (especially older adults) have lesser tendencies to experience cognitive decline when they are sociable. That's because being connected with your loved ones can decrease the levels of stress and anxiety which are one of the reasons why one experiences memory loss.

- **Feed Your Brain**

Lastly, fill your diets with food that are good for the brain and memory. (I will share with you a list of brain boosting foods in the next chapter.) If possible, make it a habit to drink supplements that promotes brain health. Some of these supplements are creatine, flavanol, gingko biloba, and omega-3 fatty acids.

Boosting your brain's function is more than using techniques to strengthen it; it also involves mental exercises as well as good habits to help you achieve an improved memory.

CHAPTER 5: 10 FOODS THAT IMPROVE THE MEMORY

Like I said, one of the best ways in order for you to combat forgetfulness and improve your memory is to include in your diet brain-boosting foods. The good news is that you don't even have to buy special kinds of foods in order to feed your brain. In fact, there could be some items already in your pantry that could improve your brain's health.

If you're interested in changing your meals into a more brain-healthy diet, then you might want to consider some of the brain foods listed below:

1. Berries

Strawberries, raspberries, blueberries—name it! Whatever kind of berry it maybe, including it in your diet can surely boost your brain's function. Berries are so nutritious for the brain that it is in fact considered as the no.1 brain food. That's because they contain *anthocyanins*, a compound that improves the brain's function to encode and restore memory, as well as its other cognitive functions.

2. Nuts

Having troubles memorizing your lessons for an exam? Why not consider munching on nuts which are rich in nutrients such as omega-3 fatty acids, vitamin E, and B complex vitamins, that are all essential for the brain's function. Walnuts in particular are found to help improve the memory, as well as prevent memory loss due to aging.

3. Avocados

Loaded with fiber, vitamins, and a good source of healthy fat, avocado is a versatile ingredient for your brain boosting meals. Not only that, this creamy fruit enables the production of dopamine, which helps improve focus and concentration, which is very important in encoding and storing memory.

4. Salmon (and other Omega-3 Fatty Acid fishes)

Fishes like salmon, mackerel, and tuna that are rich in Omega-3 fatty acids are also your best bet when it comes to brain foods.

5. Broccoli

You have to thank your mom for forcing you to eat this green vegetable when you were young. That's because broccoli is rich in minerals and vitamins such as vitamin C, B vitamins, iron, calcium, and fiber, which are all good for your brain and over-all health. It also contains a micronutrient called choline that boosts the brain's development and also improve the memory's retrieval process.

6. Spinach

Lutein, which is another type of antioxidant can be found in the green leafy vegetable, spinach. This antioxidant helps remove toxin build-up in the brain that can cause cognitive deterioration when you age.

Besides that, a study in a university in Massachusetts shows that students who consumed a healthy amount of spinach in their diet have better comprehension and have better scores than those students who didn't eat spinach.

7. Tomatoes

The next time you eat your salad, make sure you have loads of tomatoes in them. That's because tomatoes contain lycopene that keeps the brain in top shape. It also acts as an antioxidant that helps prevent cognitive deterioration.

8. Rosemary

Shakespeare wrote in Hamlet, "There's rosemary, that's for remembrance..." that's because this modest herb has properties that help eradicate the harmful free radicals in the body that can cause damage to the brain. When you include rosemary as an ingredient to your meals, it helps enhance your brain's concentration as well as memory.

9. Coconut Oil

For years, health experts have identified coconut oil to provide loads of benefits for the body, such as prevention of heart disease, improvements in immunity, weight loss, and good digestion. Besides these things, using coconut oil to cook your meals is also beneficial for the brain health because it contains medium chain triglycerides or MCTs that improves the brain cells' function.

10. Dark Chocolate

Yes! You read that right! Consuming chocolate, dark chocolate in particular, can help improve your brain's health. In fact, one study shows that older adults who drank hot chocolate had improved memory functions that lasted for hours. That's because chocolates are proven to increase a person's ability to concentrate and focus, which are all important in encoding, storing, and retrieving memory. They also contain flavanols that increases the blood flow to the brain, which is vital for a healthy cognitive function.

Of course, even if chocolate is good for the brain you still want to consume the recommended amount of chocolate which is about a square inch per day.

Plan your meals by including these healthy foods in your diet today!

CONCLUSION

Thank you again for downloading this book, "Memory Manipulation".

Improving your memory is never too late or early, so it's important that you take the chance to strengthen your brain and sharpen your memory when you can!

Although there are a lot of reasons why you forget or could experience memory loss, it doesn't mean that you can't do anything to improve your memory. By following the tips and techniques I shared with you in this book and by having a healthy lifestyle, you will surely have an improvement in your memory over time. Remember that the brain is like a muscle, so you always have to put it to work for it not to weaken or deteriorate.

Never underestimate what your brain can do, even if you're old! The brain has a *neuroplasticity* ability which makes it adapt to changes no matter what age you are; so memory loss due to aging is never an excuse because learning and keeping your brain's health in top shape is under your control!

Prevent memory loss, improve your memory to ace that test, lessen those "tip of the tongue moments", and start exercising your brain today!

Finally, if you enjoyed this book, then I'd like to ask you for a favor, would you be kind enough to leave a review for this book on Amazon? It'd be greatly appreciated!

FREE Bonus Book**

Thinking

Positive

Daily

A Guide to Personal Growth

And Self-Esteem Mastery

Table of contents

12. <u>Passing on positive vibes to others</u>

<u>Conclusion</u>

Introduction

This book is meant to serve as a helpful guide for those people at cross-roads between surviving the past and claiming a whole new approach to life.

You see sometimes even with the most enviable family, a great career, financial freedom and great friends and relatives, without the ability to nurture a positive mindset, you find that most people still continue to live the most unfulfilled and unmotivated lifestyles.

Look around you and especially take a deeper glance at those people in your immediate circles; your friends, relatives and even co-workers. Do they seem somehow stuck regardless of how much bliss they have going on in their lives? Do you find yourself wondering why they accept how things are and move on like all is just fine. You see those hitches you found while analyzing who they really are on the inside, this could be the same outlook you project when they look at you.

A positive approach to life means that you dare to believe in good things during bad times, that you choose to be grateful for what you already have and not keep lamenting on what you still lack. It's about depending on 'you' to bring forth positive actions and feelings; that you know you have the ultimate power to make you happy and content.

In this book, not only are you going to learn how to look at the glass half full rather than half empty, but you will also learn how to accept life's limitations without surrendering to them. So if you know that life is a gift, why should you limit yourself and keep you from maximizing your potential?

Life is too short to live in a shell of negativity and limitations! Continue reading and hopefully this book is able to shine on some enormous insights on your thinking and offer a whole

new positive approach to life.

Chapter 1

Developing a positive mental attitude and its benefits

Still stuck in the past?

Did you know that without your due consent, no one can make you inferior? One of the most compelling ways to increase the chances that you'll reap success is breeding a positive mental attitude. This positive approach towards life makes you much happier, and the easiest person you and other people can relate to becomes you.

So you've been through some rough patches in the past, terrible things have happened, you've been shaken and torn but that's in the past. You see you cannot afford to start living your life on automatic pilot. By embracing a positive overall mindset, you are able to change the odds and especially break the chains of emotional slavery.

What is a positive mindset?

This means choosing your reality and how things work out and affect you by maintaining a positive mindset. Ever wondered how some people despite the challenges they go through still manage to remain happy while others keep agonizing over their circumstances?

This is because one of them opted for life and its fullness and because they understand that their thinking today determines not just where they are today but where there will be tomorrow.

The power of positive thinking

Optimistic people are in a better position to handle the changes that are inevitable in life. For example most people develop severe illnesses as they age and it is those with a positive mindset that are able to face such challenges and go on living.

A positive mindset determines how it is that we deal with loss, pain or disability. Take a look at Nick Vujicic; that guy has literally had to live the most challenging life but has emerged with an inspirational story. Born without limbs, instead of looking down on his disability, he has taken the initiative to become an inspiration by living his life without limits.

The beauty of embracing a positive mental attitude is that you are able to adapt to changes and challenges that confront you and even go an extra mile of serving as an icon of inspiration. Even when the angel of death comes knocking, a person with a positive mental attitude is able to confidently soldier on and instead of leaving behind sad memories, his/her positive vibrations are able to tap on precious memories, laughter and dear reminisce to be treasured for many, many years.

How to build a positive mindset

If you choose to adapt positive mental attitude as a way of life, it no doubt brings forth constructive changes into your life. While you may not be in the position to change your challenging situation right now with either your job, family or where you live, you can choose to approach life with positivity. This can be achieved by challenging such negative thoughts and improving your overall outlook on life.

So how do you build a positive mindset?

i.   **Identifying those negative thoughts**

To be able to prescribe medication, a doctor must first find the culprit. The first step towards controlling your thoughts is breeding awareness. You can try keeping a journal of the way you perceive different things. This means your work, environment, school, family, parents, friends and everything else around you. This will help you to pay attention and listen to that inner voice in your head. Awareness is where the healing begins.

ii.   Using positive affirmations

Words carry so much weight; we use them to build ideas, conversations and sentences in paragraphs. How much positivity do you reaffirm with the words exiting from your mouth? While the words you utter are first shaped by the thoughts that you harbor, the more you utter positive words the more positive you render your thoughts.

Make it a pursuit of wellness to commit to positive thinking by embracing positive language habits. Our choice of words says a lot about our attitude and our thought patterns. When you replace your negative words with positive ones such as "I love myself", "I am a conqueror", "I can do it" and such, then you begin tapping on positive vibrations.

iii.   Focus on the present

Bearing in mind that everyone has problems, this perception comes in handy when practicing a positive mental attitude. Did you know that the things you worry about their happening almost never happen at all? In most cases, even if these things that worry you end up happening, they often don't end up being such mighty problems as you'd have anticipated.

The point is that if you quit worrying about tomorrow and focus on today, you can easily minimize such worries and fears that often breed negative thoughts.

iv.   Who are your friends?

You know the people that you choose to surround yourself with should be able to rub positive vibrations on you.

It is therefore really important that you make the conscious choice of spending time with those people who spell positivity, are supportive and who energize you.

Remember a drowning victim will not only impact negatively on you, but you can bet he'll take you down with him when his little shaky comes crumbling down.

v.   Challenges? No, Talk of opportunities!

A wise person uses the bitter bricks that life throws at him and uses them to lay a firm foundation. Instead of allowing challenges and problems to get the better of you, turn them into open opportunities to make you better.

Remember what happens to you highly depends on your approach. Often, the difference there is between a dismal failure and a successful outcome is just a mild shift with your perception. How we respond to situations, particularly how we respond to challenging situations determines the ultimate outcome.

Choosing to see challenges as opportunities communicates a person with a healthy mark of self-confidence, optimism and openness not to mention an adventurous spirit.

vi.　Don't compare yourself with others

It's sad how most people waste precious time comparing themselves and their situations with other people. I mean why compare yourself with other people if you know there is not a single person in the world that can do a better job of being you than you can?

Comparing yourself with other people often leads you to become judgmental of you and respectively harboring negative thoughts. In comparison, there can never be a win. In fact, if you must compare yourself, you can try using your past and present situation instead of basing the comparison on others.

Think of the sick in hospital, think of the disabled and many other less unfortunate in the society. Instead of trying so hard to be someone else, start counting your blessings and you'll realize that there is no better person to want to emulate than yourself.

vii.   Know You are not Perfect

It is true everyone wants to feel in complete control of everything around them. That's a lot more like trying to be a god or goddess. While you are not perfect, it would be timely to stop pursing perfection and simply accept that the tides will not always sail the way you govern.

Sometimes things will happen unalarmed, sometimes they will get out of control so instead of draining your energy on negative emotions, just accept that today things didn't go as planned and look out to a better dawn.

Chapter 2

Attracting good vibrations

Feeling good about yourself will help you to attract good towards you. You see like when you wake up in the morning feeling so thankful for a new day instead of reminiscing on your problems? Confess things like "I had such a good night sleep", "I feel great!" or "It's sure going to be a great day for me".

It is with every feeling, every thought that we build the energy that vibrates and radiate around us. Your most dominant vibration be it positivity or negativity attracts quite an equal share of the same from the external environment.

According to the law of attraction, you have the utmost choice to attract what you want and shun away what you don't want and that only happens when you are in touch with surrounding vibrations.

Respectively, as you choose to consistently encourage positive, uplifting thoughts, your life greatly improves in every aspect. The trick is to opt for such thoughts that feel incredibly nice, concentrate and live them as these are the ones that help attract positive vibrations from the rest of the world.

Positive self affirmations

What are you saying about yourself? Did you know that positive statements and affirmations highly condition the subconscious mind to ultimately help develop a more positive perception of you? Positive self affirmations are the complete opposite of a self-accusing attitude.

But what are affirmations really?

These are positive thoughts often in first person present tense with references like "me", "myself", "I" which when said and repeated over and over to yourself become engraved to the point that they define you. You don't necessarily have to say them out loud; they can be a whisper, written down or you could simply allow them to linger in your mind though unspoken.

How to positive affirmations

Let's see, where is it that you get these affirmations from? Affirmations are easy to create and practice. Affirmation should work to help you change for the better. Here's an easy method to start creating positive personal affirmations:-

Identifying those negative beliefs

This is best done in handwriting rather than electronically. Get a pen and paper where you create two columns right and left. On the left column, make a list of all the self-limiting statements that you've been using on yourself. Even better spend a few days listening closely to you.

What negative things are you saying about yourself? While jotting down every negative self-talk that comes to your mind, make sure you've not left out any statement no matter how insignificant it may seem.

Create affirmations from those beliefs

So you already have your list of those negative beliefs, compiling that must have been hard and harsh. The next part isn't about to be any easier as we will now be writing some new statements. While these negative beliefs have surfaced for the longest time possible, you will no doubt encounter discouragement and resistant forces, you'll probably even feel like its weird altogether. On the right side of your paper, write a new affirmation that transforms the negative one stated into a positive.

For example, a statement like "I am hopeless when it comes to love" becomes "True love is about to knock on my door, and am so ready!" Make sure the statements are in present tense and don't forget to use baby steps, even Rome wasn't made in a day.

Start practicing the new affirmations

At this point, your left hand column is already replaced with the positive affirmations, so make sure the negative beliefs get toasted.

With just the positive affirmations at hand, designate a strategic location around the house at an area where you frequent. It could be over your kitchen's sink or above your toilet paper roll, these areas are impossible to miss on a daily basis. This helps you gain limitless access to your affirmations.

However, there is no need to dwell too much on them as they should only serve as an occasional reminder that your thinking is undergoing transformation. Whenever you catch yourself saying or thinking negative beliefs and thought s, use these affirmations to make a turn around.

Start Living in these affirmations

Like they say, practice makes perfect. Now the most important part of this attitude transformation process is that you get to live the part. Now that you've already started practicing the affirmations, you have started believing in them, you realize how things start to change and for the better.

Eventually, the negative statements will have gradually disappeared from your mind. This is because once you start saying these positive affirmations, you start hearing them, when you start hearing them, you start believing and eventually when you believe, things start changing. In essence, if positive affirmations are going to be realized in you, you will have to be bold enough to begin now.

Affirmations you can embrace daily

In essence, self-acclaimed affirmations tend to be so absent in our lives; in our culture, our environments especially. While they may seem as just simple messages, how they can change your life is impeccably awing.

These affirmations helps in not just re-programming your thought patterns but also ultimately changing the way you approach situations and reason out. If you want to be this happy and successful person, you need to embrace a fiercely positive and motivated approach to life.

You need to get rid of those negative, self-defeating beliefs and positively program your subconscious mind. Here is a list of positive affirmations you can incorporate in your life to help make you a better person.

Affirmations when angry

- I choose to forgive myself; I am responsible for my own life.
- I choose to remain calm even when facing challenges.
- I choose to speak my mind and not allow frustrations to build up in me
- I choose to channel my anger to productivity and not self destruction.

Affirmations when afraid

- I refuse to let my courage be shaken by fear

- I choose peace and love instead of fear

- I live life courageously, I have no fear

- The future looks promising and I will be successful

Affirmations when feeling sad

- I choose to be happy under all circumstances.

- I am not allowing self-pity get in the way of my joy

- It is during my greatest solitude that I am most fruitful

- Self-pity is not an option, I choose to be happy

Affirmations when you've lost hope

- I choose to see the good in everything around me

- I refuse to give up; I am more than a conqueror

- I may not clearly understand the situation, but there's going to be a lot of good in the end.

- I am a fighter; no mountain is too high for me.

Chapter 3

Getting rid of negative people and start attracting

positivity

Defining the toxic People

These are those 'friends', colleagues or relatives who you know

does everything to make your life miserable and nothing to

help build you. They tend to shun away constructive ideas,

opinion and change so they remain stuck in their situations

without the insight to see beyond what they are battling.

You see those people who take centre stage in your life, those

people that you call your friends, have you stopped to think

how it is that they impact on your life? It is true that friends are a precious gift, but the moment one of them turns toxic, then no doubt it is time to let them go.

People can be toxic in so many ways; there are those who will try to belittle your ambitions and those who will try to lead you towards destruction. However negatively someone impacts on you, the time to let them go is now! Know that great people do the complete opposite, they are the ones that make you feel great about yourself and help fuel your dreams and aspirations.

Why it is important to detox your life of negative influence

You see negativity affects not just you but everyone else around you. However, the best thing is that you always have a choice to make. If you make the decision to remain positive and back that up with action, then you start encountering positive people and situations. The people you choose to surround yourself with should be those that instead tap in positivity and growth. Here's why you need to get rid of toxicity from your life:-

- **It slows you down**- Negative people never have goals or objectives in life. They in turn discourage you from pursuing your dreams. In essence, they slow you down any way they can and before you realize it, you are sailing together with them in a miserable boat of self-pity and unfilled dreams.

- **They drain your energy**- You see that precious energy that you would have been invested into doing something constructive is instead wasted on negative, backward thinking. This negativity drains your energy so much to the point of creating stress and anxiety.

- **You miss out on great opportunities**- When negative people surround you; the possible chance that positive change will thrive is minimal, in fact very insignificant! Inwardly, their influence in your life holds you back from embracing opportunities towards success.

-

Getting rid of toxic relatives and friends

Sometimes you realize that the person bringing toxic influence to you holds an irreversible influence in terms of blood ties. It could be your mum, your sibling, your spouse or your child.

First of all, family is supposed to rule as our safe haven every time. It therefore can get really hard to accept the odds when the person bringing us the deepest heartache is someone we already treasure. So in such moments it becomes really hard to just walk away, in fact it feels like the meanest and most terrible thought. But then again while some of our relatives will build us and others toil to break us down, there's got to be that point where we draw the line. So how do you deal with toxicity from blood relatives and close friends?

a) Sometimes they are so uncaring or agonizing to you on purpose, but still you realize their way of existing forces you to compromise on your happiness and limit yourself.

   In this case, it might mean spending less time with such people, loving them from a distance or ideally completely removing you from the equation when it deems unbearable.

b) There will be those who instead of openly addressing a situation, they tend to make annoying, subtle gestures directed at you. Their idea is no doubt to get you upset. When it's a family member, try making it clear that you love and respect them, they are entitled to their own opinions and ideas and that you respect.

If they care about you, they will support you and stop with the aggression but if they persist, you might need to create some space. Never should you allow anyone regardless of how closely related you happen to be in terms of blood to subject you to emotional blackmail!

c) You only hear of bullies in school, but did you know that family members can be the biggest bullies? You need to know that with a mind of your own, no one possesses the freedom to assault or push you around. You've therefore got to have the nerve to stand up for yourself and confront these bullying minds. Remember you are your only hope of liberation in this case.

d) Keep yourself fully fueled and refuse to neglect yourself just because those people close to you do. If you find yourself in an unfortunate situation of living with a toxic person, invest quality time to rest and recuperation.

Don't allow their influence to keep you up at night thinking and questioning whether it's you doing things all wrong. They simply have issues, period! So are you going to allow them to succeed in driving you crazy?

If you realize you cannot control what they do or how they react, then make sure to take care of yourself by remaining self centered, living positively and living healthy through regular exercise, mindfulness, proper diet and prayer. Keep them agonizing on how you are able to diffuse all their venom and keep it working out for you so impeccably!

e) Incase these toxic people gets physical and you've made attempts to reconcile things, then you should already be done taking the unnecessary blows. It deems time to become the curtain raiser in this story of fate and destiny by playing the role of 'hero' in your life.

There is the law that governs humanity and you should love yourself enough to accept that until you allow such people to face the consequences of their actions, then they will only remain as impeding ghosts always in the way of the happy and more fulfilling life you deserve.

f) You can't harbor hateful feelings- You see hating a toxic relative only pulls you down to their very level. An eye for an eye will leave the entire world blind. So regardless of how unforgivable and despicable someone becomes, never allow hate to build up in your heart.

When you start hating someone it becomes you digging two sorry graves, one for the offender and one for you. In essence, the best revenge is when you choose to be the opposite of them by living well, raising your head up high and creating bliss and peace in your life.

g) Sometimes people can change- Funny enough; some people can still be repaired in the long run. You see often even after people becomes toxic and the trust that existed is broken, it is important to note that with willingness to rise above the situation, there is always hope.

All you need to do is understand that trust rises and falls over and that it takes un-waivered strength to hang on and grow together. So if there is room for dialogue and a willingness to reverse the odds from the two sides involved, then it remains an endeavor worth trying.

h) Sometimes you've got no choice but to really let go- While you cannot be in full control of how people impact on you, you can make the decision to not yield to them. With their actions and opinions constantly invading your heart and you trying to find ways to make things work, it reaches a point when enough becomes enough.

The world is not perfect and you won't be the first to let go of some long-term relationships and bounds. Don't be afraid to let go and do what feels right and what makes you happy.

By the end of the day, life is too short to keep compromising your happiness and growth for people who will never make the effort to meet you half-way the race.

Chapter 4

What is emotional baggage?

This is best defined as a negative everyday expression and approach towards life that holds on to past wrongs, disappointments and trauma. Sometimes the ghosts stem from our childhood, our upbringing or past interactions.

These past feelings and thoughts about the negative things that have happened to you in the past carries so much weight which respectively poses negative effects on your overall behavior and attitude.

Because of this emotional heaviness, you lack the zeal to seize opportunities, appreciate the good things in your life or to tap fully into your God given potential. In essence, emotional baggage limits you from living a fulfilling happy life.

Unpacking your emotional baggage

Carrying emotional baggage is like carrying a heavy load to an unknown destination. As it is, holding onto unresolved emotional feelings inside subjects your body to physical suffering and the more the emotional baggage piles, the worse the body becomes.

You need to realize that your feelings are not who you are and make the choice to rise above them. As alive as is the fear of missing out in life, so is the fear of letting go.

You see the problem is not that you have emotional baggage, but that it has come to a point that it defines you, this makes it an issue in need of immediate action.

Take your time; it calls for baby steps

However, ditching a long-held belief isn't about to be an overnight process, it will take you longer than a week, a month even an year all because it is a life-time process.

The good news however is that, it is possible. However, the challenge lies not in getting immersed in either the pain or the joys but in keeping your heart open and not constricted and barred.

Understanding that it is in the present and not the past that you can experience happiness, love and fulfillment will help deal with the fear of letting go.

While it will be a step by step process, take your time and don't spiral to the next step until you derive satisfaction that the current step is indeed working out for you. Let someone close to you in on this journey as their presence serves as assurance that you are not alone.

How to let go with steps

So is your past impeding so much on your present and possible future it surfaces like a leach that just won't let you take a breather? Having come to terms with the fact that you need deliverance and having understood that you are your own master, here's how to release and cull out emotional baggage:-

1. Make a firm decision to let go

True, you've already come to the reality that you need to let go of your negative emotions, experiences and thoughts from the past, but the decision needs not be dependent on circumstances but infinite.

This is where you say 'enough is enough' to you and make a pact with yourself that no matter what, you are either letting go or letting go!

2. Identify the dirty culprits

You see you can't deal with something if you can't fully identify what it is. Take time to analyze your life from your childhood and other significant interactions growing up. What is this that has left you wounded, scarred and painfully hurting? What was your contribution in these interactions and what makes it so hard to forget them?

Once you are able to understand how these past relationships and interactions have negatively impacted on you, then you can identify which current issues have potential to make a similar impact and cull them out.

3. What are your current triggers?

One of the greatest reasons that past ghosts keep haunting us in the present is because we continue to tolerate potential triggers.

Something that reminds you of the past and something that has the power to provoke past feelings, memories and reactions needs to be spotted and uprooted.

4. What is your reaction or approach to such triggers?

Looking back on your life, what has been your reaction to such triggers? Like for example if your emotional baggage involves your husband's infidelity, what happens when you feel suspicious or distrustful of him?

When you are feeling neglected, controlled or mistreated by him, what is your immediate reaction? Often you realize that your immediate response is over-reaction, losing your calm and anxiety.

When you are able to identify your reaction to things that trigger your past demons, you are able to make a turn around with them. Remember your attitude is a choice you make. So if you choose to not allow such triggers to define your mood, you help change past outcomes.

5. Get in touch with reality

Even when you are able to discern that your reaction to current situations is tied to the past, the feelings can sometimes be so intense it becomes hard to react any different.

Now it becomes important to identify with your present by facing the open reality. Use your subconscious mind to counter feelings and thoughts that are irrelevant today, that are not a reality today.

Say it's regarding your once unfaithful husband; do you have evidence of your current suspicions that he could be unfaithful? While the answer is definitely no, will you stop allowing inhibiting ghosts determine your future!

6. Start living in the present

Now you can choose how you want to live, react and approach life's situations. Go ahead and create positive affirmations to use every time you feel like the ghosts from your pasts are threatening to surface!

Make positive statements like "I will trust a lot more and not be afraid to live my life to the fullest". When you start claiming good things, positive things, they in turn starts happening.

Search your current life situation and sure you must be able to identify something positive and one that directly contradicts your past experience. Make this the silver lining in this dark cloud and use it to soar.

Finding the good both in your past and present helps reclaim your power where you become no longer the victim but the master of your own destiny.

Chapter 5

Life is not perfect

Let's face it; life is a battlefield and not a bed of roses. Your attitude and daily approach to life's situation should be a lot more flexible and it should remain definite to anticipate failure at times. This way instead of such situations weighing you down, you will already have an escape plan.

So when life doesn't go the way you planned, how do you react to that? Do you develop a cynical outlook? Do you become absorbed in the misfortunes and set-backs that life mercilessly throws at you? Often you realize that it is every step you take towards a 'golden future' that seems to take you two more steps backwards.

How many people today are guilty of wanting a picture-perfect successful future? A loving husband, enviable kids and a to-die-for career? Sometimes you've wanted to get rich overnight and live the most comfortable life. While forgetting that life is already beautiful even without trying to perfect it or salivating for luxurious living, we forget to actually live.

Being happy just because

You don't become happy in life because things are indeed perfect, you are only happy when you are able to look beyond the imperfections. Sometimes all you need to do is to take a step back in time and re-evaluate your attitude, how is it that you perceive things around you?

Being happy just because means that instead of living from fear, you start living from faith. That instead of dwelling on self-pity, you can start practicing compassion for others. As it is, people are going to hurt you, shake you and try to break you. Where you remain after all the drama is all that matters.

Again given that disappointments and heartbreaks can really harden your heart against trust to the point of making you question the goodness there is in humanity; know that there will always be a way out. The way out is choosing to be happy just because regardless of all life's challenges. Here are 5 reasons to want to choose happiness:-

- Choosing to enjoy the moment instead of agonize becomes a habit, it becomes character, it defines you.

- Choosing to celebrate instead of mourn highly benefits your future.

- Happiness even from just a simple smile spells improved health.

- Every new day becomes a new opportunity to become better than you were yesterday.

- You start positively impacting on other people's lives.

- You become the master of your own destiny.

Overcoming disappointments and heartbreaks

Regardless of the disappointments, hardships, adversities and pain you may have suffered in the past, there is no reason to beat yourself up. The fact is that disappointments don't discriminate unless you allow them to, heartbreaks shakes you but they don't cripple.

Say you missed out on that promotion; she turned down your marriage proposal, he cheated on you with your best friend or you missed out on that defining auction. It is through tests and challenges, disappointments and heartbreaks that we are able to savor the delicious taste of victory. The most important thing to bear in mind is that getting up after a setback is not an option, it's a definite resolution.

Here's how to keep moving forward even after life has handed you some bitter lemons.

Cut yourself some slack- You see, self-blame is often the reason why you are unable to accept the outcomes in certain life situations and simply move on. Agonizing on what you did or didn't do for things to turn out better is a complete waste of time. Just accept that it happened and move on from here.

Play the role of a spectator- This means that you avoid the drama by stepping away and shifting your attention to more positive things. This helps deal with the hard blow as you have already distanced yourself from the event. You know you might just yell out loud and say "It wasn't me" like the events were simply playing out from a movie script.

Don't make it personal- How about you target alternative explanations to the situation. It doesn't have to be something you did or didn't do; it doesn't have to be you. Look at the situation in a broader perspective and find something else to place the blame on.

Focus on your strengths- These you must have many! Think of what you are really good at, how many other things you've achieved in your life, how many other things have worked out according to your expectations. You see those skills you may have gained in the past, horn them and fight to become a better person.

Positive influence- If things are going pretty rough for you right now, it only becomes worse if you choose the company of bitter, self-centered and negative minds. Think hard about who you would turn to in a desperate situation, on impulse and let this be the person you reach out to. The naysayers, let them do what they do best, live in pessimism.

Chapter 6

Getting back on your feet after a financial setback or job loss

Failure is part of life

Sometimes we are faced with the hardest decisions to make, other times we are faced with the hardest challenges to overcome. Regardless of how many blows we receive in life, we must remain positive knowing that failure is an inevitable price while trying to accomplish something.

At one point in life, we all have experienced unexpected financial disasters. It could be that you lost your job, a medical emergency or uninsured losses. In essence we must understand that it remains impossible to predict your financial journey, financial success is never guaranteed.

The Greatest Successors once failed

Even the most successful investors got to suffer financial challenges from time to time. The point therefore isn't to invent a strategy that keeps you from falling, it's having the drive to pick yourself up and start all over.

The most compelling success stories tags along some mind-blowing hustles and setbacks which were used as foundation to success.

So are you facing financial challenges and setbacks, it feels like you have reached your dead end? Know you are not alone and that there is hope to come out stronger than you started off.

Getting Back on Your Feet

You must have already realized that finding the motivation to rise up from failure is often easier said than done. Having beaten yourself up so often even branding yourself the 'greatest failure of all time', you will need more than just inspiration to resurface. You are going to need a strategic plan; you are going to need a working plan.

So regardless of what brought upon your financial setback, know that your path to recovery will require relentless dedication and a willingness to re-prosper. Your situation isn't unique, you are not the first to walk this lane and this serves as even more conviction that you too will rise.

Here's a six-step plan to help you recover from a financial setback:-

Accept reality- So things are what they are, stop wallowing in unnecessary despair and accept the odds. It is devastating okay, totally crushing and a complete bummer, okay! The most important thing here now is that it's in the past, it's done. Instead of wasting your energy resisting a futile fact, bounce from this past and start making progressive steps forward.

Take your inventory- How much is lost? Surely, there must be something you can still savage. Take an inventory of the current situation and come to terms with the resources and the liabilities you have. You are going to need this little information when developing a come-back plan from this catastrophe.

You see in financial management, you must understand where you are today to be able to make realist future plans. Ask yourself what assets still remains, how much money you owe, how much income is still available, how much are your expected expenses and what is your credit score as at now? Are there long-term implications such as I.R.S, alimony or health issues? All this needs to comprise your recovery plan.

Define Goals and objectives

Where do you see yourself in the future financially? After knowing where you stand and your targeted destination, now you can easily plot the course there. Make sure your goals are specific with definable end results. Again they should be measurable and attainable so you are able to measure your progress as time unfolds.

You see you cannot afford to set unrealistic goals. Such goals like setting goals of becoming a millionaire within a span of 1 year after filing for bankruptcy aren't viable. Again remember that a goal that holds no deadline remains just a wishful thought. This means that you will need to be smart enough to outline a time or date that the goals are to be met.

The Big Plan

Now with all the armor you will need, the next step is to bridge the gap there is between where you are today and where you wish to be in future. While you are not superhuman, you must respect your emotions along the way because remember no one said it will be an easy road.

Now you will need to figure out the most efficient path that gets you from point A to point B with fewer hassles while not forgetting to ensure that it's rewarding and fun all through.

Take action

You see without consistent action, your goals remains void and null. Action however is what converts your goals into tangible results. This is there you repackage your experience, knowledge and skills towards accomplishing your purpose.

Correction and adjustment

You've already fallen down, picked yourself up and shaken off the dust. You've learnt from past mistakes so it's quite unlikely there will be a repeat of the same. While a wise person knows that perfection is impossible, he knows too that correction is desirable and timely.

Often, you realize that your first plan isn't always your best plan so don't even waste your effort trying to stick to plan A to the latter. Adjusting your approach along the way helps achieve your goals more efficiently and effectively.

Chapter 7

Relaxation and Fun

It is true that positive thinking in itself won't cure cancer or help reduce your weight. However, positive thinking makes it easier to reduce stress, better manage your life and take care of you.

Making time to get you engaged in enjoyable activities, reason being that they are relaxing or because they are fun and absorbing is really important. While it's easy to get buried in life's challenges or get overly focused on work, most people tend to overlook the need for fun and relaxation along the way.

Fun and positive thinking

Being gloomy all the time is not a healthy approach. Like they say "Too much work and no play makes Jack a dull boy". You therefore need to understand that to boost your positive thinking; you need to make time to unwind, letting go of your worries and cares.

Engaging in something fun and relaxing is a key aspect in helping cultivate not just positivity but also resilience, stamina and energy; a combination you are going to need when you are facing challenges or setbacks in life.

Fun and Relaxing activities to try

Making the choice to engage yourself in fun and relaxing activities gets you openly claiming that "Life is good". Why? It is because you are finding something enjoyable to look forward to and this helps replace negative motives with positive ones.

While some fun and relaxation options that works for someone else may not necessarily work out for you, you will need to find that something that gets your happiness flowing.

Regardless of what this activity is, it doesn't really matter much as long as it is able to enhance positive results overall for both your body and mind.

Here are fun and relaxation activities you can embrace to help boost your vitality:-

Meditation

This is a relaxation and fun technique that offers a soothing effect that inherently brings awareness and relaxation. As an easy activity that requires only a few minutes of your time, you should know that people who constantly engage in meditation display more positive emotions not to mention are able to lead a purposeful life.

Writing

You don't know how magical a pen and paper and the comfort of your couch can get when it comes to unwinding. You know those positive experiences you've had, why not take time to write about them.

Let go and just get immersed in the moment. Writing on positive experiences helps override any possible negative thinking and also acts as a reminder that there is still so much good in this world.

Listen to music

Amidst all those challenges and setbacks in life, dare to look back and get nostalgic with archived music. You must have heard the statement that music is food for the soul too often you already believe it.

Studies have shown that not only is music able to prompt brain changes linked to our emotions but it also abstract decision making. While everyone has their own set of music, make time to indulge in a good listen once in a while.

Exercise

The revitalizing and relaxation benefits that exercise accords are hard to ignore. In respect to a more positive attitude, exercise helps boost your energy while amazingly improving your mood too. So, at times when you feel in need of emotional uplifting, why not take a walk or hit the gym?

Charity work

Being in a position to help someone in need helps bring out the best in you. It could be a friend, relative, neighbor or a complete stranger that needs help.

Again, volunteering to work in a retirement or children's home brings forth a new approach to life. Instead of sulking in your misery, you are able to find more than a 1000 reasons to smile and keep going regardless of the blows that life throws at you.

Other ways to relax and have fun includes:-

- Taking a hike
- Getting a good massage treatment
- Working on a puzzle
- Watching inspirational documentaries
- Cooking – Trying out new recipes
- Engaging in intimacy (safe) with your partner

Chapter 8

A laugh goes a long way

Have you ever heard of someone who went to the doctor seeking treatment for stress and the doctor prescribed more laughter? Well, you better believe it!

There is no telling how far a laugh can go, from bringing people closer together to establishing amazing connections. Everything can take a complete turnaround from just a slight giggle or guffaw.

A heated argument or chilly unfamiliarity can be easily diffused by a hearty, deep laugh. So are you feeling completely run down, why not try laughing a lot more than you did before?

A Medical Approach

The laughter therapy details that you are able to change psychologically when you laugh. Through laughter, you are able to stretch muscles throughout your body, face not to mention that your pulse and blood pressure goes up. Laughter can serve as a mild work out and offers some advantages that a physical workout brings.

While laughter is also said to help burn out calories, it doesn't mean that you ditch your diet plan or stop exercising. It is a combination or laughter and relentless efforts to be better including exercise that counts.

Laughter as your best medicine

Someone is asking out loud how come laughter is said to be the best medicine. That is no doubt understandable but, are you ready to listen to facts on laughter and positive living?

Laughter is first associated with comic relief and it's impossible to not have tapped into the mood-boosting benefits of a good laugh at one point in life. While humor is infectious, roaring laughter is a lot more contagious than a sniffle, cough or sneeze.

Laughter if shared especially increases intimacy and happiness and helps bind people together. The best part in regard to benefits brought upon by laughter is that it is free of charge.

Physical health benefits of laughter

- Laughter helps relax your muscles

- Laughter also boosts your immune system

- It goes a long way to help boost your immunity

- Helps prevent heart disease

- Lowers the stress hormones

Mental health benefits of laughter

- Adds zest and oomph to life

- Improves your overall mood

- Works amazingly to enhance resilience

- Helps ease fear and anxiety

Social benefits of laughter

- Helps strengthen relationships

- Helps attract good vibrations from others

- Laughter enhances team work and cooperation
- Laughter works well in diffusing conflicts and disagreements

How to bring more laughter and humor into your life

Sure you've experienced the joy of playing with a furry friend or a pet at one point in your life. Laughter is an open gift, so natural and inborn. Have you never wondered how infants begin to smile right from the moment they come into this world?

Even though you never got the chance to grow up in a household where laughter surfaced, you must have learnt the joy of laughter at a later age. Eventually, you are able to naturally incorporate laughter in everything else that you do. However, in case it gets challenging, here's how to go about it:-

Smile- Whenever you spot something even mildly pleasing, take the rare chance and smile!

Counting your blessings- They must be a handful! Considering the good things happening around you distance you from negative thoughts.

Move towards laughter and humor-Often times, people are happy to share something humorous no matter how ancient for the very reason that it gives them a chance to laugh again. When you hear laughter, seek to know what's that funny reason as to why the laughter and indulge yourself.

Spending time with funny people- There are those people that laugh easily sometimes at themselves, other times at life's absurdities. While their playful view of laughter can be contagious, surround yourself with such people.

Cultivate humor- No; you don't have to be Mr. Bean to be able to crack a joke. Cultivating a joke can be as easy as seeking to find out funny things that have happened around other people, and there, you can easily find something to laugh about.

Chapter 9

The power of Exercise towards clearing and renewing your mind

The Inevitable Hassles

You see there are those days that you simply find yourself going off-course. The workload is unbearable with calls and emails streaming in, with constant interruptions disrupting your actions and your thought process, the pace can deem frenetic.

With the speed you are moving at, you are bound to feel sloppy and unproductive leaving you edgy and stressed out. Many are the times you'll end up feeling like you missed out on something, like you've somehow lost touch with a certain part of your life.

You know like you go shopping for everything you have in the house only to realize that you've gone a little bit over the top with your budget when you get to your house. This frenzy shouldn't be left to escalate so much to the point that the only thing you do when you get home is yelling at the dog and snapping at your kids. It is therefore important to find a way to stay under control during such frantic moments,

Mind De-clutter

If you've gotten familiar with computer terminologies, then you must have heard of Random Access Memory (RAM). This is the storage in a computer that determines the processing capacity of a computer. It so happens that the more applications your computer runs the more RAM it utilizes and the slower it gets. Surprisingly, the same case applies to your brain. Well, have you ever heard of brain de-cluttering? This means clearing your mind of all the 'garbage' that inhibits your peace and laxity. In addition to your daily responsibilities, you still have to face the demands of pending errands, upcoming holidays, and unbearable moods with your boss not to mention having to cope with negative thoughts building up from life's frustrations.

With so much that needs your attention, it is only normal for your mind to go into overdrive with all the worries and endless commitments. Regardless of life's hardships, one thing that remains constant is that life goes on. The best give you can give you is taking quality time to clear your mind. You neither has to spend so much time on this as just 10 minutes a day are enough to help reboot your brain and recharge your energy.

You see when you decide to stop worrying, ruminating and planning too much and simply empty all that suffocation baggage from your mind; then you begin to live. It is now that you realize how much you've allowed yourself to live in limitation, it is now that you are able to prove yourself as much wiser than your problems.

Positive thinking, positive attitude, positive actions, positive resolutions, positive living! Each one of these goes hand in hand with the other.

Exercise and Relaxation

Apart from meditation and writing, physical activity is another incredible way to help clear your mind and reclaim your energy. True you might figure that having been running up and down in the office and around the house is already enough to get your blood pumping.

However, without forgetting that such work and house routines are the main culprits as to why you are feeling beat, it would be senseless to consider any form of walking within these parameters as healthy.

Separating yourself from the causative action and away from the immediate chaos helps your mind tune into a new environment. Exercise comes in uncontested as one of the most defining ways to help clear your mind.

Look at it this way; how comes you tend to think so much better when you exercise or take a walk? You see not only does exercise enhance your cognition due to improved blood flow, research also shows that the critical part of the brain involved with the learning and memory is most active during exercise.

Again, exercise has repeatedly been cited to be a cure for inexhaustible health conditions today ranging from diabetes, depression, Alzheimer's disease, memory loss, blood pressure and more. Respectively, when it comes to sleeping better, exercise works incredibly amazing on your brain to facilitate good sleep so you can now say goodbye to sleepless nights when you engage in exercise and physical activity.

What kind of exercise?

Now you already know that you don't have to wait for those feel-good feelings to come by accident as you can bring them to life by exercising. It doesn't have to be just the physical; you can also try mind exercises too. Here are exercises both mind-oriented and physical that you can incorporate in your day to day schedule to garner an overall healthy and positive mindset:-

Mind Exercises

- **Meditation** -This can be termed as a brain exercise that works by calming the nerves. Through meditation, you are able to focus on a single thing and with practice; you end up being able to pull your thoughts back every time they start to wander off.

- **Cooking lessons**- The decision to learn how to cook a foreign cuisine works incredibly fine. You see cooking uses a number of senses including smell, sight, touch and taste which are a great boost for the brain to maintain healthy functionality.

- **Music**- This simply says it all. You could try taking music lessons on a particular musical instrument. A piano has such a relaxing and mind blowing impact not to mention that being able to make music solely from your brain is a great way to relax and unwind.

- **Breathing exercises**- Breathing falls a lot more on meditation but on its own, the ability to master individual breathing techniques brings forth open-minded clarity that tags along transcendence.

Physical Exercises

- **Walking**- This is one of the safest and easiest physical exercise that anyone can try. A 30 minute's walk a day helps boost stamina while also lowering blood pressure, heart disease and diabetes risks.

- **Running**- This exercise while adhered to in moderation helps boost your heart rate and improve your bone health. Today there are many open arenas to try out this sport and if done as part of a group or with a friend, the derived results are exemplary.

- **Swimming**- This is a low-cost workout that helps pamper the whole body while improving flexibility too. However, don't forget to use sunscreen if swimming outdoors.

- **Dancing**- Another readily available type of exercise to consider. Dancing to such music trends as Jazz, Hip-hop and Latin American music can be a great way to exercise not to mention are incredibly fun too.

Chapter 10

Daily discipline

Ideally, life goes more smoothly and is more fulfilling when we embrace a positive mindset. How great would it be if you would make it your unaltered initiative that before going to sleep you get to consider what was right and wrong on that day and use this to improve yourself?

On this note, you realize that the decision to elevate your mind remains definite. One of the ways you can achieve this mind elevation target is appropriating for emotional, mental, physical and spiritual needs on a daily basis.

Such small actions you overlook daily are the ones that greatly impact on your health, productivity and happiness. The commitment to nourish these critical domains in your life could lead to you to finding purpose and passion in life while making you a better person overall.

Here are five major disciplines which if incorporated in your day-to-day activities will help highly elevate your state of mind:-

i. **Practice gratitude-** Nothing compels positivity better than a grateful soul. Make it a habit to write a gratitude list each passing day. This not only helps boost positive thinking but also helps look forward to better days ahead.

ii. **Keep yourself active-** Ideally, if you want to remain at your best, exercise cannot be a luxury. Not only does it help nourish your cognition but it also helps slow cellular aging too. Knowing how much further exercise can impact on your overall wellness makes it a daily disciplinary call of action.

iii. **Eating healthy-** Lest we forget that what we eat is what we become. Nurturing your body through healthy eating helps nurture your life too. This ensures that you bask in vitality and energy in abundance. Again a healthy body posture also boosts your overall self-esteem and confidence respectively welcoming positivity and bliss into your life.

iv. **Embrace integrity-** This means you choose to live in alignment with good morals, values and character. Practicing integrity living ensures that by the end of the day, you are able to trust and respect people not forgetting boost your overall self-esteem. Everything else that follows only spells positivity and good living!

v.   **Spiritual nourishment-** We all need to have spiritual nurturing to be able to remain inspired and resilient. Take some time therefore on a daily basis to nourish your spirit. This may be through prayer, meditation, yoga or through any other means that tallies with your spiritual belief.

Being thankful at all times

Sure you've heard this phrase a lot especially from the spiritual books. That you should be grateful for the simplest things, no matter how insignificant they may seem. You shouldn't wait for life to indulge you in practical lessons to start appreciating life.

If you are to keep yourself happy, you need to start doing what is right for your spirit. Start by assessing your relationships, career and spirituality and pinpoint where you could be feeling dissatisfied and why. Follow that up with working on what needs to be done to regain balance and facilitate the motivation needed by you to make changes. This will help nourish those domains that are starved for attention while fostering the overall personal environment necessary for your life to thrive.

How do you feed your spirit?

Doing what you love

It would definitely be great to have a career that is simply aligned with your passion and ultimate goals. While we can't always have this satisfaction, it s important to pursue a career that leaves you in a happier mood even though not necessarily perfect!

That means if you are unhappy with your job, don't wait for that to bring you at a battle field with negative emotions. Instead, do some soul searching and know what it is that appeals to you with no limitations then make every effort to pursue that vision wholeheartedly.

Prayer

Pray and not just for you but for someone else too. You see prayer means seeking guidance and favor from the supernatural God, the one that is above all in majesty and power. Surrendering your entire self to God and letting known your needs and supplications, helps unburden your soul and recharge your body.

The aspect of believing also goes a long way because as the Bible says, if we pray and believe then it's done! The beauty there is in prayer is that we are able to let go of emotional burdens and find new strength to start all over. Prayer remains a key aspect in spiritual nourishment.

Practicing Appreciation

Many are the times that something good happens in life and we end up perceiving it as norm. In fact, many are the times that we miss the chance to be grateful for the good things in life and instead find ourselves agonizing in the negatives and disappointing part of life. However, if you learn to see life as a gift, then you will learn to appreciate those simple things like having a roof over your head or a plate of food on your table.

The power of intuition

Ever heard someone confess of a wary feeling just before something bad happened? Many are the times that we dismiss our intuition and interpret is as simple fear or anxiety. Needless to say, being able to listen and act on your intuition helps you avoid unnecessary and unpleasant hassles.

That means if something doesn't feel right to you, make it an ultimatum to avoid it regardless of how much others advocate for it. Remember your life is just yours to live and the responsibilities from your actions will never be shared!

Chapter 11

Positive thinking and your self esteem

Working on your Self Image

What does your outlook say about you? Does it outline someone who knows their self-worth? Someone who walks with their head held up high? Someone who isn't afraid to explore their options? Someone who is not afraid of failure but is rather afraid of not trying? You must know that self worth isn't self-absorption; it is rather relentless self –respect.

Self confidence is vital and is applicable in almost every aspect in all our lives. Sadly, most people still struggle so much to nail it and this greatly inhibits their success. You see when you have confidence; you tend to inspire the same in others.

However, if you are going to accomplish a positive self-image, it will have to start by pursuing positive affirmations about you. So again, what are you really saying about yourself? Are you branding yourself as incompetent, shy and a slow learner? Well, that is exactly what you become. Remember that you tend to reap what you sow!

Never put yourself down

There will always be those self-accusing voices in your head. Those that say you are not good enough, that you don't fit in and that you are destined to fail. However, how your life turns out is not dependent on these negative accusations; it is dependent on what your subconscious mind says about you.

In the light of day, when you are thinking sane and are saying things out loud, listen carefully to what you are saying. Make sure that every word you are firmly upholding is a diamond that shines over all those accusing voices in your head. Learn to engage yourself in positive self-dialogue.

Remind yourself everyday of the potential and integrity you possess. If you make it a point to feed on a positive mental diet, then your character and personality sync in positive vibrations too.

Whenever you hit the road, make sure to walk with your head held up high. Not with a conceited attitude though but with self-pride that comes from knowing your worth.

Confidence from positive thinking

Often, it is such negative thoughts and negative self affirmations that cripple your self confidence. No one is to say how long it will take you to reclaim back your self-esteem but what remains constant, is that the journey towards that achievement must start now!

There are many ways to change self-criticism and negative thoughts. However, focusing on all of them at once may deem harsh and overwhelming.

The best approach therefore is to tackle them one at a time, working on each individually and assessing the outcomes regularly. As they say, practice makes perfect so make it a habit to observe regular practice through thought replacement.

Where you'd be inclined to make a negative statement or self-affirmation, replace the same with a positive ultimatum. Make sure to mean what you say, make sure to own up to every counter statement you use on your negative thinking.

Self Confidence is a Necessity

Self confidence comes in handy especially in most potentially difficulty situations such as making a speech, asking someone out on a date, playing a competitive sport, socializing on unfamiliar grounds or speaking up in a crowd.

The good news is that by thinking realistically about a certain situation, regarding you on a positive light and using simple anxiety management techniques can help boost your confidence.

Confidence is often a blend of both self-esteem and self-efficacy. Self esteemed is more related to holding a belief that we are good enough and deserving to live a happy life. Self efficacy on the other hand is the internal belief, or sense that we are able to accomplish various goals and tasks we face in our lives.

Each one of these goes with the other. Someone who has self-confidence thinks positively about the present and the future while on the other hand someone who lacks confidence carries a negative perspective in regard to his / her potential and future hopes and dreams.

Tips on improving your self esteem

Luckily, while you may not possess that admirable self-confidence that leaves you assured of tomorrow, you can always improve on it. Here are tips that you can use to help boost your overall self-confidence:-

1. Stop listening to your inner critic, in fact, stand up to this inner voice gagging up any destructive thoughts.

2. Motivate yourself positively. This means when that inner voice screams just how sloppy you are, counter that accusation with an affirmative action that spells how meticulous you are.

3. Learn to self-appreciate yourself. There's sure got to be something about you to be proud of. Like how you are may be able to make people laugh, how thoughtful you can be or how well you are able to impact on other people. These positive assurances help neutralize negative mood and in the long-run works towards building self-esteem.

4. Write your attributes down. By the end of the day, take time to reflect on you and outline those things that makes you appreciate you. The best thing about writing down these attributes is that even after weeks have passed, you can read them again and again to the point they become affirmed.

5. Doing the right thing greatly help raise your self esteem. An action as simple as getting up from your comfort zone at the couch and hitting the gym or choosing to understand a certain situation other than being judgmental is a plus.

6. Quit trying to be perfect, no one has ever been! Perfectionism is a great culprit of low self-esteem. It can paralyze your ability to live life to the fullest. The procrastination you have leaves you afraid of failing, of not living up to your set standards and this makes your self-esteem sink with quite a pace.

7. Accept that mistakes and failure are part of live. That along the way you will stumble and fall and that it's normal, that it's okay. The secret is to ensure that you remain your own best friend through thick and thin.

8. Be kind to others. How you treat others is often how you treat yourself and how they possibly treat you in return. If you practice more patience and kindness with others, this becomes a bold realization of positivity and in return you reap the same in double portions

Chapter 12

Passing on positive vibes to others

Our Daily Interactions

On a daily basis, we interact with different people. Some impacts positively on us while others negatively. Our concern however is how to tap into positivity. You see positive vibes can easily be picked up from those around us, the immediate environment and even from animals.

However, you need emotional quotient to be able to grasp these vibes and inherently absorb them. EQ (Emotional quotient) is thereby your ability to process emotional details most especially those involving assimilation, understanding and perception.

Have you never met someone whom though a complete stranger at the moment, deep down you cannot deny the fact that you already do like them? That they being in your life add cheer, you like their company so much and you keep looking forward to hanging out with them?

Training Your Mind to Recognize Good Vibes

These people who appeal to you just by mere intuition, these are the people who make you smile regardless, they add zeal to your life, they are the ones who emit positive vibes.

Here's how you can train your mind to recognize these good vibrations from other people:-

1. **A genuine smile**- From just looking at a genuine smile from someone, you'll be able to tap on the same and ultimately fill your heart with happiness.

2. **Eye contact**- When a person smiles at you, make eye contact with them. Eyes are able to emit respective vibes whether positive or negative. Depending on your EQ, you will be able to define the perceived vibrations.

3. **The tone of the voice** –You should know that this carries a vibe too so listen carefully to how they speak and the tone they use.

4. **Body language** -While listening to their words and paying close attention to even their body language, you'll be able to pick up the vibes, the positive ones.

Positive Vibes vs. Negative Vibes

The first thing you need to understand is that you have a choice every time. Whether to be at peace with yourself or to be in resistance is your choice.

Coherently, you tend to attract positive energy when you are at peace and create negative vibes when in resistance. While it's a just a simple choice, most people still choose to sail in negativity.

The truth is that, regardless of how many setbacks and challenges we face, how we perceive them is what determines our respective attitude. It is not your boss, the traffic, parents or colleagues but your very perception that creates negative energy and stress.

While circumstances are neutral, you tend to generate positive vibes if your inner self is in congruence instead of being resistive.

How to Attract Positive Energy

Remember that we are magnets. Every time we emit positive energy in terms of feelings, vibrations and thoughts, we attract more positivity to us.

Respectively, when we dwell in the negatives, we attract negatives that work awfully by sapping our strength and energy in the process too.

If you really want to attract wellness, vitality and health to yourself, you must stop circulating toxic, thoughts and feelings.

Here are 8 ways in which you can attract positive energy into your life:-

i. **Choose to start your day with meditation-** The art of meditation helps you create a sound awareness with your surroundings.

All you need to do is just relax and allow yourself to feel your consciousness in the midst of emotions and thoughts. Meditation always has such impacting power in helping create positive vibes all day long.

ii. **Love yourself enough-** This means that despite your flaws, you learn to love and accept the person you are and keep reminding yourself of those great qualities you possess.

iii. **Forgive your past failures and disappointments** – The person you were yesterday can only make you a better person today. You will therefore need to stop engaging in guilt and self blame from past happenings. Decide that today is the first day of the rest of your blissful life and revel in it.

iv. **Stop controlling others** – Know you will never be at peace if you remain self-consumed and selfish. You need to let go of your insatiable need to control. Every time you try to control a life's situation, you end up feeling frustrated respectively generating negative emotions.

If life is more like a raging fire in itself, what purpose does it serve to struggle putting it off? Instead, find ways to let go and allow yourself to surface. This way you will not only attract the gracious incentives of life but you will also attract and retain positive energy.

v. **Envision a Peaceful life-** While your mind might already be addicted to negative thinking, you will need unmonitored motivation to break out and start attracting positive energy.

Stay alert and conscious and you'll witness your mind churning out fearful emotions, stress and anxiety. You will be surprised how intensely positive vibrations will flow.

vi. **Tomorrow isn't promised** – You will need to stop worrying about the future because like they say, tomorrow isn't promised, not for anyone! You achieve absolutely nothing by worrying; in fact, your worrying becomes a complete waste of precious time.

Just incorporate practical planning and leave the rest to fate and destiny because no matter how much you try to fight, whatever that has to happen will happen. When you stop worrying you cull out negative emotions and leave room for positive vibes to thrive.

vii. **Laughter is food for the soul**- Don't just laugh, keep laughing and don't stop! Indulge in activities that provoke humor such as watching funny movies or sharing jokes. This way, you will be laughing your way back to healthy living by shunning negative thoughts and embracing positive vibes.

viii. **Bask in the wonders of nature**- You see nature has a way of awakening such positive vibrations you never knew existed. Sit down for a moment and envision yourself watching the sunset, sitting by the ocean or hiking in nature.

Can you already feel the peace and assurance that comes from such moments? Taking time to get immersed into the wonders of nature helps quiet your mind and body. This way not only do you get to tap into positive vibes; you also find a way to connect with a deeper part of yourself you never had the chance to explore before.

Conclusion

Thank you so much for downloading this book.

I hope the content herein has managed to serve as enlightenment towards positive thinking. I hope through the tips and in-depth information provided in this book, you will manage to garner a more positive approach to life.

Remember there is nothing as compelling as being able to positively impact on another. On that note, if indeed the book has been helpful to you, please do not forget to extend the bliss. It would be sad if someone close to you missed the chance to benefit from the content in this book as much as you have.

Thanks again and good luck in everything!

CPSIA information can be obtained
at www.ICGtesting.com
Printed in the USA
FFOW01n0954230116
20771FF